Patricia Aguilar Talamante

The use of artificial intelligence in academic work

Patricia Aguilar Talamante

The use of artificial intelligence in academic work

ScienciaScripts

Imprint

Cover image: www.ingimage.com

This book is a translation from the original published under ISBN 978-613-9-40369-1.

Publisher:
Sciencia Scripts
is a trademark of
Dodo Books Indian Ocean Ltd. and OmniScriptum S.R.L publishing group

120 High Road, East Finchley, London, N2 9ED, United Kingdom
Str. Armeneasca 28/1, office 1, Chisinau MD-2012, Republic of Moldova, Europe
Printed at: see last page
ISBN: 978-620-7-63736-2

The use of artificial intelligence in academic work.

Table of Contents

Introduction.......... 3
Theoretical foundation.......... 4
Generative artificial intelligence in university teaching.......... 6
SWOT analysis for the definition of faculty teaching activities using ChatGPT... 7
Strengths.......... 7
Opportunities.......... 8
Weaknesses.......... 8
Threats.......... 8
Here are some jobs that can be developed with Artificial Intelligence.......... 9
Within the advances in AI in the public sector, Elizabet (2024) mentions:.......... 10
AI presents the following challenges:.......... 11
Most applied types of artificial intelligence today (Maria, 2024).......... 14
Expert systems.......... 14
Artificial Neural Networks.......... 16
Deep learning.......... 19
Robotics.......... 22
Intelligent agents.......... 24
Advantages and challenges of artificial intelligence types.......... 26
Expert Systems.......... 26
Artificial Neural Networks.......... 26
Deep Learning.......... 26
Robotics.......... 27
Description of the method.......... 30
Results and discussion.......... 31
Conclusions.......... 42
Bibliography:.......... 43

Introduction

The growing influence of artificial intelligence (AI) has permeated different areas of knowledge and society, arousing a growing interest in its application, characterized by the rapid adoption of tools and systems based on artificial intelligence, not being Public Accounting the exception, the usefulness of this tool has had a significant impact on higher education, offering innovative solutions to improve the efficiency and effectiveness of teaching-learning processes and methods, from virtual tutoring systems to automated assessment platforms, AI is transforming the educational experience not only by providing new forms of personalization, feedback and access to educational resources, but also the academic practices of university students. In this context, it is essential to explore the perception and attitude of students towards the use of artificial intelligence as a tool in the completion of their academic work, the interaction between AI and education raises relevant questions about ethics, intellectual autonomy, the originality of the work done, the quality of the information used by AI and of learning itself. The present study is situated at a time of educational transition, where the convergence between technology and education is redefining the paradigms of teaching and learning, where we seek to analyze the opinion on the experiences of university students in relation to the use of artificial intelligence in their academic activities, in order to better understand the challenges and opportunities that this phenomenon presents in the educational field.

Theoretical foundation

Artificial intelligence refers to the ability of machines to mimic human behavior and perform tasks that would normally require human intelligence, advances in processing power, machine learning, and the availability of large data sets have driven the development of AI in various sectors (Elizabeth, 2024).

Artificial intelligence is a constantly evolving field and is being used in a variety of applications, from speech recognition and vision to healthcare and logistics (Górriz et al., 2020). Currently, AI is being researched and developed to improve efficiency and accuracy in a variety of fields, such as education, finance, academic and research paper creation, at the moment they cannot be differentiated from human-made work, neither in human review nor in anti-plagiarism platforms, and as their use expands, ethical and legal concerns also arise, such as privacy, security, and impact on employment (Maldonado, 2023).

In this sense, Abou-Foul et al. (2023) mention that this new technology is having a great impact on academic and research work, helping data collection, which allows researchers to devote more time to its interpretation and analysis. Likewise Chiu et al. (2023), asserts that artificial intelligence is having a great impact on the academic field, as it has the potential to improve teaching, research and academic administration. However, Adams et al. (2023), in their research, indicate that there are concerns about the negative effects of artificial intelligence on academic work and research.

Some people argue that artificial intelligence cannot completely replace the human ability to think critically and be creative. Moreover, they suggest that its use could encourage plagiarism and lack of originality (Gendron et al., 2022), despite these debates, there is no doubt that artificial intelligence has come a long way in text writing, as is the case with ChatGPT (Zhang & Li, 2021).

It is important to highlight that students use artificial intelligence as a tool that can restrict their development of critical thinking. Sometimes, they use the information without a deep analysis, which leads to hasty conclusions. Therefore, the importance of the teacher's role in guaranteeing an objective, responsible and ethical use of this technology is emphasized (González, 2023).

It is essential to ensure that both teachers and students receive the necessary training and support to use artificial intelligence effectively in education. This involves providing them with adequate training to become familiar with the various tools available and understand how to integrate them effectively into the teaching and learning process (VERA, 2023).

Generative artificial intelligence in university teaching

In recent years, the development of generative artificial intelligence techniques is reaching a level of maturity that was unthinkable a decade ago.

These advances have given rise to tools that make it possible to generate images from natural language descriptions, perform automatic transcriptions and translations in real time, or interact with a conversational assistant capable of generating formal and technical documents.

Based on a SWOT analysis, this article contains a series of reflections on ChatGPT, a chatbot that in November 2022 revolutionized the world of generative artificial intelligence by solving mathematical problems, generating source code, creating stories or producing news and technical reports.

What challenges does the irruption of tools such as ChatGPT pose for university teaching? What opportunities does it offer to improve the quality of teaching? Are we facing a turning point in education as we know it? (Luis Jiménez Linares, 2023).

SWOT analysis for the definition of faculty teaching activities using ChatGPT

Source: ChatGPT: reflections on the irruption of generative artificial intelligence in university teaching (Luis Jiménez Linares, 2023).

Strengths

Despite having delved into the underlying technology of ChatGPT and having received feedback from a variety of users who have highlighted its limitations, it is not all downsides to using this tool. At present, its main advantage lies in its accessibility and availability. ChatGPT can be accessed from any web browser, making it a lightweight tool for users, who do not need to install any software on their devices or have advanced computer skills to interact with the tool from any device. In addition, it is available twenty-four hours a day, seven days a week and is free to use (although a paid version has recently been launched that offers greater availability and faster response time). The only limitation in its use is related to the overload of requests in the free version. Therefore, it is possible that when trying to access ChatGPT, you may not be able to interact with it because it is currently being used by thousands of users. However, the recent paid version promises to resolve these availability issues.

Opportunities

The Spanish proverb suggests that if you can't beat the enemy, join him. This perspective poses an interesting challenge for the teaching community: to turn ChatGPT into an ally to help students acquire the competencies defined in the curricula. Undoubtedly, this represents a challenge, as no previous generation has had such powerful tools in their academic experience.

Weaknesses

The revolution unleashed by ChatGPT since its launch suggests that this model, with more than 170 million parameters and continuous training with a growing corpus of data, seems to lack significant weaknesses. However, this is far from certain. Widespread use by users from a variety of disciplines has revealed the model's current weaknesses.

Threats

Due to the great success ChatGPT has had since its launch and the variety of applications that have been found for it, some inappropriate uses have also arisen that could harm the context in which this tool is used.

Here are some jobs that can be developed using Artificial Intelligence

- Financial risk analysis: Use ChatGPT to analyze financial data and forecast potential risks to a company. You can train the model to recognize patterns associated with accounting fraud, liquidity risks or compliance issues.
- Automated accounting advice: Develop an automated accounting advice system using ChatGPT. This system could provide answers to common questions about taxes, financial accounting or audit reports.
- Financial decision evaluation: Use ChatGPT to simulate different financial scenarios and evaluate the impact of business decisions, such as investments, mergers and acquisitions, or changes in accounting policies.
- Financial reporting: Trains ChatGPT to generate financial reports based on accounting data. This could include generating financial statements, financial analysis reports or audit reports.
- Financial trend analysis: Use ChatGPT to analyze financial trends in historical data and predict possible future scenarios. This could include identifying trends in financial markets, analyzing macroeconomic risks or predicting cash flows.
- Environmental and social risk assessment: Trains ChatGPT to analyze sustainability reports and assess environmental and social risks associated with business activities. This could include identifying risks related to climate change, corporate social responsibility or environmental compliance.
- Accounting policy generation: Trains ChatGPT to generate

basic accounting policies based on internationally recognized accounting standards, such as International Financial Reporting Standards (IFRS) or Generally Accepted Accounting Principles (GAAP).

Within the advances in AI in the public sector, Elizabet (2024) mentions:

- Process automation: It has enabled the automation of routine tasks in the public sector, such as document processing, data management and customer service. This has improved efficiency and freed up resources for other more complex activities.

- Data-driven decision making: It has facilitated decision making in the public sector by analyzing large volumes of data and extracting relevant patterns and trends. This has enabled more accurate planning and efficient resource allocation.

- Improving public services: It has improved the quality of public services by providing personalized recommendations, optimizing public transportation, predicting disease outbreaks, and improving public safety, among others. Now, regarding some advances in AI in the private sector:

- Customer experience: Companies use AI to improve customer experience through chatbots, recommender systems and sentiment analysis. This enables faster and more personalized customer service, improving customer satisfaction and loyalty.

- Business Process Automation: In the private sector it has been used to automate repetitive tasks and improve operational efficiency. This has led to cost reduction and increased productivity in various industries.

- Innovation and product development: AI has driven innovation in the private sector by enabling the development of smarter products and services; from autonomous vehicles to virtual assistants, AI has transformed entire industries and generated new business opportunities.

AI presents the following challenges:

- Ethics and liability: Artificial intelligence raises ethical issues, such as privacy, algorithmic bias and liability in case of wrong decisions, it is essential to establish ethical and legal frameworks to guide the development and use of AI.

- Job displacement: While AI can improve efficiency, it also raises concerns about job displacement; strategies need to be developed to mitigate negative impacts on workers and facilitate the transition to new skills and occupations.

- Security and Cybersecurity: AI can be vulnerable to malicious attacks and manipulation. Efforts are required to ensure the security of AI systems and protect sensitive data, as well as more specialized personnel in the field.

- Excessive surveillance: As AI has functions to monitor workers, privacy tends to be violated, so it should only exist for a certain degree of management.

- Health: AI systems can favor the care and improvement of health at work, identifying risks, predicting accidents before they occur, but they also carry health risks derived from implementing new systems with AI, where it is convenient to have updated existing regulations and procedures, as they can be subject to cyber-attacks.

- Responsibility: When implementing AI technology, if errors occur in the organization due to the decisions made by the AI systems, determining who is responsible will be a complicated issue because the question will be whether the developer of the AI system, the implementing employer, or someone else involved is responsible.

"Artificial intelligence has transformed the public and private sector, providing opportunities to improve efficiency, decision-making within the world of work and the quality of services; however, it also presents significant challenges that must be adequately addressed; it is critical to establish a sound ethical and legal framework, invest in education and training, and foster collaboration between the public sector, the private sector and the academic community to maximize the benefits of AI and mitigate its risks. Lack of digital skills could hinder the progress of any society, while encouraging investment in training, closing the gender gap, flexible and hybrid work environments that foster empathy and concern for working people could contribute to improving the quality of the work environment, as well as the growth of each person collaborating within any institution, whether public or private, keeping them updated and improving their skills and competencies" (Elizabeth, 2024).

In the European AI Regulation it is based on a risk approach. four types of risks are identified (Judith Arnal, 2023):

• **Unacceptable risk.** AI models that have been categorized as such, because they affect the safety, life or rights of people, will be banned outright. By way of example, social scoring models, biometric identification in public places or toys with voices that invite dangerous behavior will not be allowed.

• **High risk.** They will be qualified as high risk models:
AI models in products covered by product safety regulations (e.g., toys, elevators, cars, airplanes and medical devices).

AI models in products in one of these areas: critical infrastructure, education and vocational training, secure components of products, essential public and private services, law enforcement that may interfere with fundamental rights, migration, asylum and border control management, and administration of justice and democratic processes.

In these cases, AI systems will be subject to stringent requirements before they can be launched on the market: adequate risk management and mitigation systems, traceability of results, clear and adequate user information, high level of robustness and security, etc. In addition, systems will continue to be analyzed throughout their life cycle.

Limited risk: minimum transparency obligations will be established.

Minimal risk.

The position adopted by the European Parliament on June 14, 2023 introduces changes to the European Commission's proposal, in particular, it broadens the scope of application of the Regulation, incorporates new definitions and structural principles for all AI systems, establishes a specific regulation for foundational models, introduces relevant changes to prohibited and high-risk systems, establishes the obligation for generative AI systems to disclose that content has been artificially generated, intensifies measures to support innovation and modifies certain aspects of the sanctioning regime.

Most applied types of artificial intelligence today (Maria, 2024)

Expert systems

Expert systems are one of the simplest forms of artificial intelligence and, although we are generally unaware of it, they are technologies that accompany us all the time and are part of our daily lives.

These technologies can be defined as tools built to solve specific tasks in the same way that human reasoning would. As you can imagine, they are known as such because they are designed for specific functions and tasks that require a good level of subject matter expertise, just as would be required of a human agent.

It works by structuring rules that tell the machine what decision to make in a given scenario. This makes complex systems very accurate, but they have difficulties in solving unforeseen problems.

Examples of the use of expert systems in business

Inventory control. These tools are ideal for inventory control, as they only need to follow numerical rules and control the stock to manage the availability of goods.

Merchandise evaluation. Some tools are built to detect damaged products or production failures through simple rules.

Business planning. By relying on rules, expert systems can forecast the results of a decision making process, as well as the risks of an investment or project.

Application of expert systems in different fields

Medicine: In the medical field, expert systems are used to diagnose diseases, design personalized treatment plans and provide clinical recommendations based on medical data and patient symptoms. For example, IBM Watson Health has developed expert systems to help physicians diagnose and treat cancer.

Financial Services: In the financial sector, expert systems are used for risk analysis, fraud detection, portfolio management and investment decision making. Large financial institutions such as JP Morgan Chase and Goldman Sachs use expert systems to optimize their operations and improve the accuracy of their financial forecasts.

Technology: In the technology industry, expert systems are applied in areas such as virtual assistance, optimization of computer systems and detection of security vulnerabilities. Companies such as Google, Microsoft and Amazon use expert systems in their products and services to improve user experience and increase operational efficiency.

Manufacturing: In the manufacturing industry, expert systems are used for process control, predictive maintenance and supply chain optimization. Companies such as Toyota and Siemens use expert systems to improve the quality of their products and increase the efficiency of their manufacturing operations.

Education: In education, expert systems are used to personalize learning, provide instant feedback and help students identify areas for improvement. Educational platforms such as Khan Academy and Coursera use expert systems to deliver educational content tailored to the individual needs of each student.

Artificial neural networks

Artificial neural networks are a type of computational intelligence algorithm that overcome some limitations of expert systems (such as their inability to solve new cases or cases outside their programming rules). Their operation is based - as in the human brain - on small units of information that, in collaboration with others, process information.

Their main function is to allow machines to extract new information from the information fed to them, in order to learn from it. For this reason, the processes that these technologies carry out are commonly known as machine learning. This allows the machine to progressively optimize its functions, offer better results and work efficiently.

These algorithms are really popular and generate a great impact on business, since they make it possible to analyze information automatically and obtain some trends, statistics or predictions on a specific topic.

Examples of the use of artificial neural networks in business
Customer care. While some chatbots only work through defined rules, there are some customer care solutions that operate through neural networks to provide more personalized and useful answers to solve customer demands.

Process automation. Artificial neural networks make it possible to delegate simple tasks to machines, automating production processes, decision-making or consumer evaluations.

Content creation. You have probably already seen that you can create copy with AI. Systems based on artificial neural networks have also proven to be effective as a tool for rewriting texts, improving images and photographs, among many other tasks. You can take advantage of these technologies to make your content more impactful.

Modern applications of neural networks

Neural networks are widely used in various fields today, being applied in a variety of sectors. Here are some examples of modern applications of neural networks and well-known brands working with them:

Technology: In the technology sector, neural networks are used for image recognition, natural language processing, machine translation and improving user experience. Companies such as Google, Facebook, Amazon and Microsoft use neural networks in their products and services, such as Google Photos, Facebook's DeepFace, Amazon Alexa and Microsoft Translator.

Healthcare: In the healthcare field, neural networks are used for medical diagnostics, medical image analysis, drug discovery and genomic analysis. Large pharmaceutical companies such as Pfizer and Novartis, as well as renowned hospitals such as Mount Sinai Hospital in New York, use neural networks in their research and medical practices.

Automotive: In the automotive industry, neural networks are used in advanced driver assistance systems, traffic sign recognition, autonomous driving and supply chain optimization. Companies such as Tesla, Audi, Toyota and Ford are using neural networks to develop autonomous vehicles and improve safety on the road.

Finance: In the financial sector, neural networks are used for risk analysis, fraud detection, portfolio management and market trend prediction. Large financial institutions such as JP Morgan Chase, Goldman Sachs and Morgan Stanley use neural networks in their daily operations to improve decision making and optimize their investment strategies.

Entertainment: In the entertainment industry, neural networks are used for content recommendations, personalization of user experiences and creative content generation. Platforms such as Netflix, Spotify, YouTube and Twitch use neural networks to deliver personalized recommendations and improve user satisfaction.

Deep learning

Deep learning is a type of artificial neural network algorithm that, as its name suggests, is deep. But what does this mean?

Deep learning refers to algorithms with a high level of complexity that allow more complicated tasks with high computational requirements to be carried out. These technologies stand out for having a complicated code and for being fed with extensive databases. That is why deep learning generally goes hand in hand with data mining, a statistical discipline that seeks to find patterns in huge volumes of information.

These technologies are ideal for carrying out more complicated tasks, but especially for performing activities that transcend the capabilities of human agents (or for which no personnel or time is available).

Examples of the use of deep learning in business

Financial estimation. Beyond the analysis of business numbers, deep learning algorithms help to assess the financial behavior not only of a company, but even on a global scale. This helps make better business decisions and understand market volatility.

Marketing. One of the most important tasks of a company is to evaluate and predict consumer behavior in order to design the best acquisition strategy. This is something that deep learning does perfectly, as it can evaluate the behavior of large volumes of customers.

Security. Because deep learning systems adapt by processing data, they are ideal for managing the computer defenses of websites and servers. They also work in the authentication of personnel and clients.

Modern applications of deep learning

Here are some examples of modern Deep Learning applications and well-known brands working with this technology:

Technology: In technology, Deep Learning is used for speech recognition, facial recognition, natural language processing, machine translation and creative content generation. Companies such as Google, Facebook, Amazon, Microsoft and Apple use Deep Learning in their products and services, such as Google Assistant, Facebook's DeepFace, Amazon Alexa, Microsoft Translator and Siri.

Healthcare: In the healthcare field, Deep Learning is used for medical diagnostics, medical image analysis, drug discovery and genomic analysis. Major pharmaceutical companies such as Pfizer, Novartis and Roche, as well as renowned hospitals such as Mount Sinai Hospital in New York, use Deep Learning in their research and medical practices.

Automotive: In the automotive industry, Deep Learning is used in advanced driver assistance systems, traffic sign recognition, autonomous driving and supply chain optimization. Companies such as Tesla, Audi, Toyota and Ford are using Deep Learning to develop autonomous vehicles and improve safety on the road.

Finance: In the financial sector, Deep Learning is used for risk analysis, fraud detection, portfolio management and market trend prediction. Large financial institutions such as JP Morgan Chase, Goldman Sachs and Morgan Stanley use Deep Learning in their daily operations to improve decision making and optimize their investment strategies.

Entertainment: In the entertainment industry, Deep Learning is used for content recommendations, personalization of user experiences and creative content generation. Platforms such as Netflix, Spotify, YouTube and Twitch use Deep Learning to deliver personalized recommendations and improve user satisfaction.

Robotics

Robotics is a computational branch independent of artificial intelligence, which has been significantly nurtured by these digital resources. This has led to a large number of robotics solutions being driven by artificial neural networks.

Today there are robots capable of walking, doing complex tasks and even playing chess thanks to computer vision systems, learning algorithms and code that allows them to make decisions. Artificial intelligence is behind it all.

In business, there are some cases of use of these technologies, especially in the area of production and customer service.

Examples of the use of robotics in business

Logistics. Robots play an important role in the management of warehouses and distribution centers. Such is the case of Amazon, which employs robots in its facilities to manage the shipment of goods.

Production. Robots have a long way to go in production, but today they promise even more advantages because they can identify damaged goods, correct errors and perform tasks that are impossible for a human worker to do.

Customer service. In some countries, especially in Asia, the use of robots for customer service has become very common. Such is the case of robots working in restaurants taking orders and delivering orders.

Modern robotics applications

Here are some examples of modern robotics applications and well-known brands working with this technology:

Industrial automation: In the manufacturing industry, robotics are used to perform repetitive and hazardous tasks in production environments. Companies such as Fanuc, ABB, KUKA and Universal Robots are leading manufacturers of industrial robots for assembly, welding, painting and material handling applications.

Medical assistance: In the healthcare field, robotics is used to perform minimally invasive surgery, physical rehabilitation and assist people with disabilities. Companies such as Intuitive Surgical, Medtronic and Ekso Bionics develop surgical robots and medical assistance devices to improve precision and efficiency in the treatment of patients.

Space exploration: In space exploration, robotics are used for research and data collection in extreme off-Earth environments. Space agencies such as NASA and ESA (European Space Agency) use robots such as rovers on Mars and robotic arms on the International Space Station to perform exploration and maintenance tasks.

Logistics and warehousing: In the logistics and warehousing sector, robotics is used to automate storage, picking and packing processes. Companies such as Amazon, Ocado and Boston Dynamics use autonomous robots and automated systems to streamline operations and increase efficiency in the supply chain.

Domestic services: In households, robotics are used to perform domestic tasks such as cleaning, pet care and home security. Companies such as Robot (creators of Roomba), Dyson and Ecovacs Robotics develop domestic robots to help people in their daily activities.

Intelligent agents

Finally, I will tell you about one last type of artificial intelligence technology known as intelligent agents.

As their name suggests, these systems have the ability to make decisions and act on them through reasoning similar to that of human beings. This means that intelligent agents must possess a good margin of autonomy and freedom to learn and execute decisions.

These technologies are currently under development and promise to make the management of business tasks easier. However, their use today is reserved, as they involve major ethical considerations.

Examples of the use of expert systems in business

Personal assistants. These are tools that can autonomously manage a person's schedule, recommend places to visit or even make decisions regarding their health.

Logistics. Through simple rules, data mining and learning, there are technologies that can find the best distribution route and even manage deliveries autonomously.

Modern applications of intelligent agents

Intelligent agents are artificial intelligence systems that can perceive their environment and make autonomous decisions to achieve specific goals. Here are some examples of modern intelligent agent applications and well-known brands working with this technology:

Virtual assistants: Virtual assistants such as Apple's Siri, Google Assistant, Amazon Alexa and Microsoft Cortana use intelligent agents to understand and respond to user requests. These intelligent agents use natural language processing and machine learning techniques to provide accurate and useful responses to user queries.

Recommendation systems: Platforms such as Netflix, Spotify, Amazon and YouTube use intelligent agents to recommend personalized content to users. These intelligent agents analyze users' browsing history and preferences to provide relevant recommendations for movies, music, products and videos.

Chatbots: Companies use intelligent agent-based chatbots to provide automated customer support through websites, messaging applications and social networks. Companies such as Zendesk, LivePerson and Intercom use intelligent agents to answer frequently asked questions, resolve customer issues and route inquiries to the appropriate departments.

Monitoring and control systems: In industrial environments, intelligent agents are used to monitor and control complex systems, such as power plants, power grids and manufacturing processes. These intelligent agents can detect anomalies, predict failures and take corrective action to ensure the safe and efficient operation of systems.

Autonomous navigation: In robotics and autonomous vehicles, intelligent agents are used for autonomous navigation in dynamic and unknown environments. Companies such as Tesla, Waymo and Uber use intelligent agents to interpret sensor data, plan routes and avoid obstacles while driving autonomously on roads and in urban environments.

Advantages and challenges of artificial intelligence types

Expert Systems

Efficiency and availability

Limited flexibility and dependence on human expertise

Artificial Neural Networks

Machine learning and nonlinear data handling

They require large amounts of data and are a "black box".

Deep Learning

Complex data management and continuous improvement

Need for large amounts of data and computing power, and are a "black box".

Robotics

Automation of physical tasks and work in hostile environments Limited cost and flexibility

Intelligent Agents Automation of digital tasks and personalization Privacy and complex interactions

Fields of application of the types of artificial intelligence:

Expert Systems

Expert systems are computer programs designed to emulate the reasoning and decision making of a human expert in a specific domain. These systems use knowledge bases and logical rules to solve complex problems. Some prominent applications are:

Medicine: They help in the diagnosis of diseases and the choice of treatments.

Engineering: They assist in the design and optimization of systems.

Finance: Provides investment recommendations and risk management.

Artificial Neural Networks

Neural networks are computational models inspired by the functioning of the human brain. They are composed of layers of interconnected nodes (artificial neurons). Their applications include:

Computer vision: Object detection, facial recognition and image segmentation.

Natural Language Processing (NLP): Machine translation, chatbots and sentiment analysis.

Forecasting and classification: Weather forecasting, product recommendations and data analysis.

Deep Learning

Deep learning is a subcategory of neural networks that uses multiple hidden layers to learn complex representations of data. Its applications include:

Industrial automation: Process control, predictive maintenance and production quality. Bioinformatics: Gene sequence analysis and protein structure prediction. Autonomous driving: Image processing and decision making in autonomous vehicles.

Robotics

Artificial intelligence in robotics focuses on creating autonomous machines capable of interacting with their environment. Some notable applications are:

Industrial robots: Automation of assembly lines and repetitive tasks.
Service robots: Hospital assistance, cleaning and customer service.
Exploratory robots: Space, underwater and hazardous environment exploration.

Intelligent Agents

Intelligent agents are programs that act autonomously in an environment to achieve specific objectives. Their applications are diverse:

Search agents: Route optimization, schedule planning and problem solving. Game agents: Chess, Go and video games. E-commerce agents: Product recommendations and personalization.

Description of the method

The present research was carried out by means of the quantitative and cross-sectional method, where the universe of study were the students of the accounting degree of the accounting department of the University of Sonora with the objective of knowing the perception and attitude of the university students towards the use of artificial intelligence in the realization of their academic work, For data collection an instrument (questionnaire) was used which was developed with the application forms and were sent to different groups for response, of which we received 124 surveys that were answered and which is considered the sample for this research, from the data obtained a descriptive analysis was made. A descriptive analysis was made of the data obtained, where we had a Cronbach's Alpha of .772, with which we can affirm that we have a 77.2% reliability in the data to be able to infer.

Results and discussion

Of the study population, 64.5% are female and 35.5% are male, of which their ages are 18 years 25.0%, 19 years 20.2%, 20 years 7.3%, 21 years 9.7%, 22 years 16.1%, 23 years 5.6%, 24 years 2.4%, 25 years old 1.6%, 26 years old or older 12.1%, of whom are in their first semester .8%, second semester 49.2%, fourth semester 5.6%, fifth semester 1.6%, sixth semester 8.1%, seventh semester 3.2% and eighth semester 31.5%.

Q1.- Do you think that using artificial intelligence to carry out university work can improve the quality of your projects?

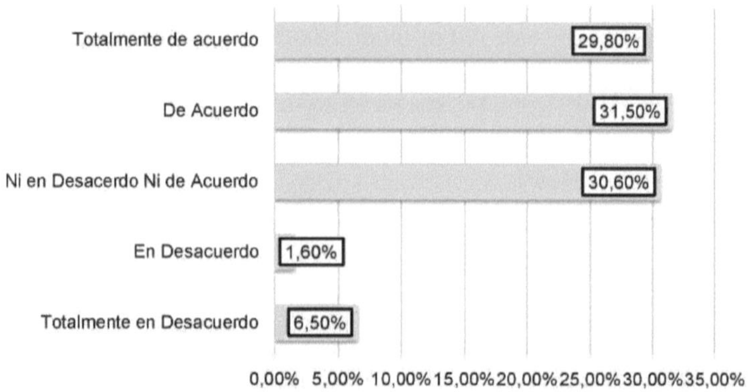

Source: Author's own elaboration.

There is a significant trend in the opinions, where a part agrees with the idea that using artificial intelligence can improve the quality of university projects (61.3%), there is also an unremarkable percentage that disagrees or even disagrees with this statement (8.1%), however, there is a considerable proportion of people who are at the midpoint of the Likert scale, 30.60% indicate that they neither agree nor disagree with the statement. Acceptance of the idea of using artificial intelligence to improve the quality of university projects is high compared to outright opposition. However, the group that is undecided or neutral is also considerable. The question reveals a diversity of opinions on the use of artificial intelligence in improving the quality of university projects, with a slightly positive inclination towards this idea, but with a significant part of the population still unconvinced or hesitant about it.

Q2.- Do you think artificial intelligence can help you save time in researching and gathering information for your academic work?

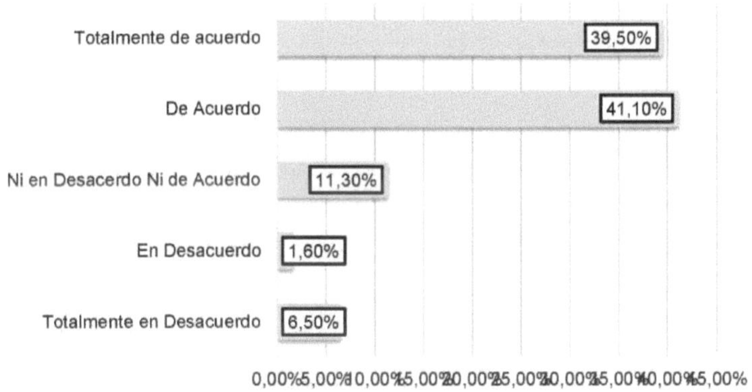

Source: Author's own elaboration.

A clear majority can be observed that agrees or strongly agrees with the idea that artificial intelligence can help save time in research and information gathering for academic work (80.60%), although the majority is in favor of the statement, there is a minority that shows some opposition or doubt about it (8.10), a not insignificant segment of the surveyed population (11.30%) does not show a definite position. The question reveals a mostly positive tendency towards the idea that artificial intelligence can be beneficial for saving time in research and information gathering for academic work.

Q3.- Do you have confidence in the ability of artificial intelligence systems to produce quality academic content?

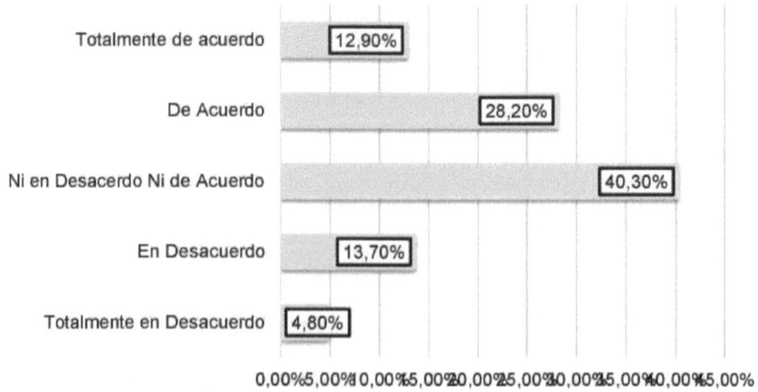

Source: Author's own elaboration.

There is a significant proportion of people who show some degree of confidence in artificial intelligence systems to produce quality academic content. However, this confidence is not overwhelming, with only 41.10% and approximately 40.30% of respondents falling in the midpoint of the Likert scale, suggesting an indecision or lack of certainty about the ability of artificial intelligence systems to produce quality academic content, however, there is considerable lack of confidence in the ability of artificial intelligence systems to produce quality academic content (18.50). The question reveals a general tendency toward distrust or hesitancy regarding the ability of artificial intelligence systems to produce quality academic content. Although there is a portion of the population that shows some confidence, this is not dominant and there is a significant proportion that disagrees or is undecided in this regard.

Q4.- Do you feel comfortable using artificial intelligence tools to generate parts of your university work, such as summaries or data analysis?

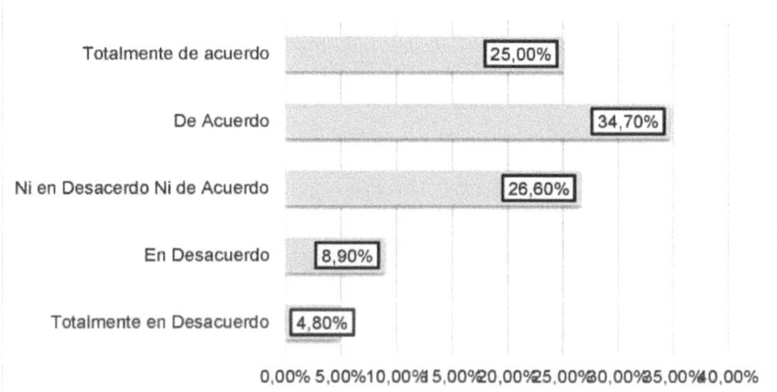

Source: Author's own elaboration.

There is a general trend towards the willingness to use artificial intelligence tools to generate parts of university papers. This is evidenced by the fact that 59.70% of the respondents are in favor of the question, although the majority show a positive disposition towards the use of artificial intelligence tools in generating parts of university papers, there is still a not insignificant proportion of people who express some discomfort or disagreement with this practice, 13.70%, a considerable segment of the surveyed population (26.60%) does not show a clear position. The question reveals a majority tendency towards a willingness to use artificial intelligence tools to generate parts of university work, although there is also a significant proportion that shows some discomfort or hesitation in this regard.

Q5.- Do you consider it ethical to use artificial intelligence to create academic papers, as long as the source is properly

cited?

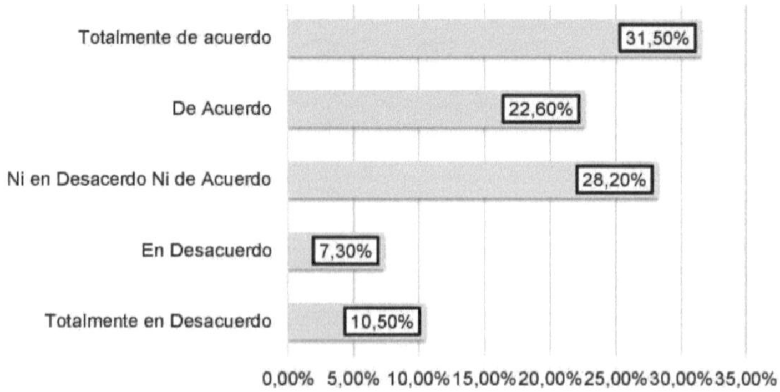

Source: Author's own elaboration.

There is a general tendency towards ethical acceptance of the use of artificial intelligence to create academic papers, as long as the source is properly cited (54.10%), although the majority shows ethical acceptance, there is still a significant percentage of people who do not agree with this practice, even when the source is properly cited (17.80%), A considerable segment of the surveyed population (28.20%) does not show a clear position. The question reveals a majority tendency towards ethical acceptance of the use of artificial intelligence to create academic papers, as long as the source is properly cited. However, there is still a significant proportion that disagrees with this practice, even under conditions of proper citation, and another group that does not show a clear position on the matter.

Figure 6. QIA6.- Are you concerned about the possibility that the use of artificial intelligence in the

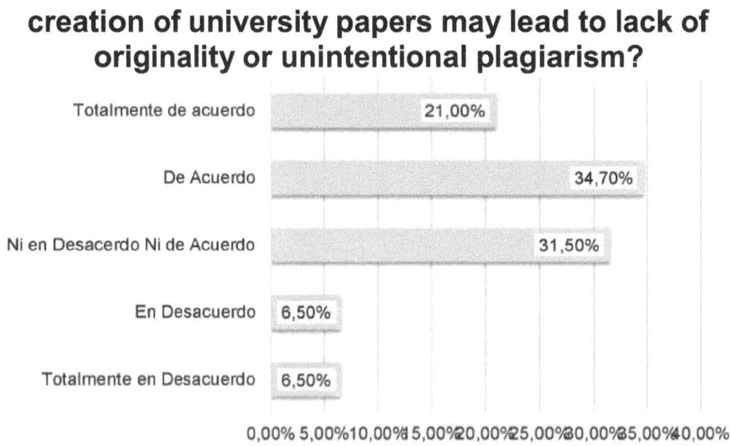

Source: Author's own elaboration.

There is considerable concern about the possibility that the use of artificial intelligence in the creation of university papers may lead to lack of originality or unintentional plagiarism (55.70%), although the majority shows concern, there is also a significant percentage of people who are not concerned about this possibility (13.00%), a considerable segment of the surveyed population (31.50%) does not show a clear position. The question reveals a majority tendency towards concern about the possibility that the use of artificial intelligence in the creation of university papers may lead to unintentional unoriginality or plagiarism. Although there is a significant proportion that shows some lack of concern in this regard, another considerable group does not show a clear position in this regard.

Figure 7. QIA7.- Do you think that professors should establish clear policies on the use of artificial intelligence in academic work?

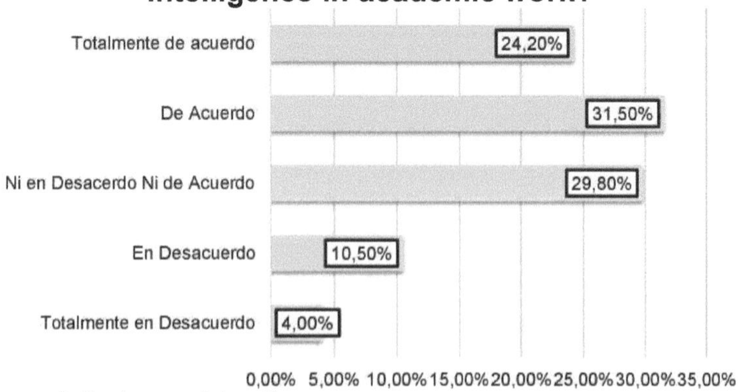

Source: Author's own elaboration.

There is a general tendency towards the idea that professors should establish clear policies on the use of artificial intelligence in conducting academic work (55.70), although the majority shows agreement with the need to establish clear policies, there is also a significant percentage of people who do not completely agree with this idea (14.50), a considerable segment of the surveyed population (29.80%) does not show a clear position. The question reveals a majority tendency towards the idea that professors should establish clear policies on the use of artificial intelligence in conducting academic work, although there is also a significant proportion that does not completely agree with this idea or does not show a clear position on the matter.

Figure 8. QIA8.- Do you think that the use of artificial intelligence in the creation of university jobs can level the playing field for students with different abilities and resources?

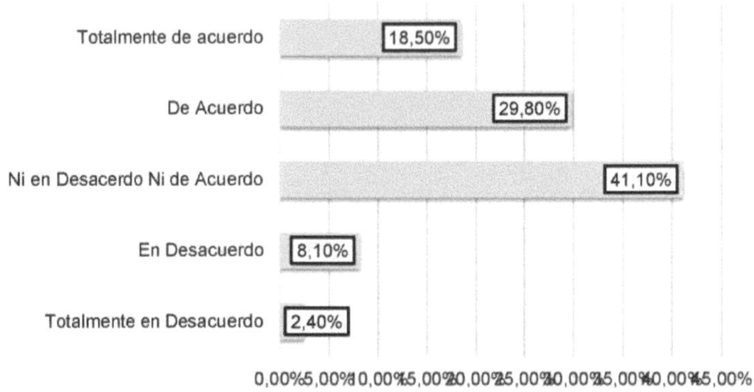

Source: Author's own elaboration.

There is some ambiguity or lack of consensus on whether the use of artificial intelligence in creating college jobs can level the playing field for students with different skills and resources (70.90%), although the majority does not show a clear opinion, there is a significant percentage of people who agree with the statement (48.30%), a minority shows some opposition to the idea that the use of artificial intelligence can level the playing field for students with different skills and resources (10.50). The question reveals a lack of clear consensus on whether the use of artificial intelligence can level the playing field for college students with different skills and resources. Although there is a significant proportion that does not show a clear position, however, there is also a considerable portion that agrees with the idea, although not overwhelmingly, and a minority that opposes it.

Figure 9. QIA9- Would you like to receive additional training on how to use artificial intelligence ethically and effectively in your academic work?

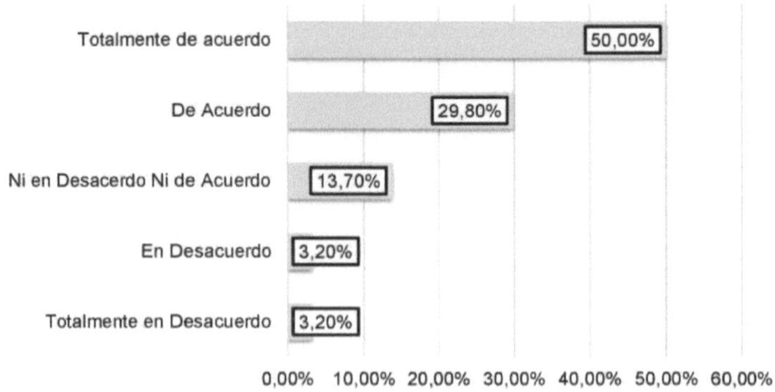

Source: Author's own elaboration.

There is a strong interest on the part of the respondents to receive additional training on how to use artificial intelligence ethically and effectively in their academic jobs (79.80), only a small minority shows disagreement or lack of interest in receiving additional training on this topic (6.40), a moderate segment of the surveyed population (13.70%) does not show a clear position. The question reveals a strong desire on the part of the respondents to receive additional training on how to use artificial intelligence ethically and effectively in their academic work. Although there is a minority that shows disagreement or lack of interest, the majority shows a high degree of interest in this type of training.

Figure 10. QIA10.- Do you think that the use of artificial intelligence in university work should be subject to specific regulations by the educational institution?

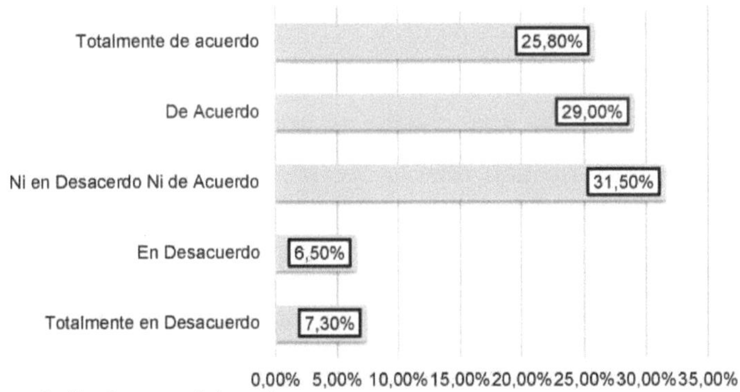

Source: Author's own elaboration.

There is a lack of clear consensus on whether the use of artificial intelligence in the performance of university work should be subject to specific regulations by the educational institution (57.80%), although the majority does not show a clear opinion, there is a significant percentage of people who agree with the statement (54.80), a minority shows some opposition to the idea that the use of artificial intelligence in the performance of university work should be subject to specific regulations (13.80%). The question reveals a lack of clear consensus on whether the use of artificial intelligence in the performance of university work should be subject to specific regulations by the educational institution. Although there is a significant proportion that does not show a clear position, there is also a considerable part that agrees with the idea, although not overwhelmingly, and a minority that opposes it.

Conclusions

There is a positive, though not dominant, inclination toward the idea that AI can improve the quality of scholarly projects; however, significant concerns and doubts persist about the ability of AI to produce quality scholarly content. Ethical acceptance of the use of AI to create scholarly works seems to be conditional on proper citation of the source, although most seem to agree with this ethical practice, however, there is concern that the use of AI may lead to lack of originality or unintentional plagiarism in scholarly works, which leads us to establish clear policies on the use of AI in scholarly works, although not unanimous and however, there is no clear consensus on whether the use of AI can level the playing field for students with different abilities and there is strong desire among respondents for additional training on how to use AI ethically and effectively in their academic work, the present research provides an overview of the diverse opinions and attitudes towards the use of artificial intelligence (AI) in improving the quality of university projects.

AI is permeating our society as ICT's did in their time, the process of maturity in its use is already in process, let's hope in the future the correct use, and that the benefits do not go to the detriment of our society.

Bibliography:

Adams, C., Pente, P., Lemermeyer, G., & Rockwell, G. (2023). Ethical principles for artificial intelligence in K-12 education. Computers and Education: Artificial Intelligence, 4.

Abou-Foul, M., Ruiz-Alba, J. L., & Lopez-Tenorio, P. J. (2023). The impact of artificial intelligence capabilities on servitization: The moderating role of absorptive capacity-A dynamic capabilities perspective. Journal of Business Research, 157.

Chiu, T. K. F., Xia, Q., Zhou, X., Chai, C. S., & Cheng, M. (2023). Systematic literature review on opportunities, challenges, and future research recommendations of artificial intelligence in education. Computers and Education: Artificial Intelligence, 4.

Elizabeth, R. R. (May 13, 2024). www.cielolaboral.com. www.cielolaboral.com: https://www.cielolaboral.com/wp-content/uploads/2023/06/ruiz_news_cielo_n6_2023.pdf

González, M. A. (2023). Responsible use of artificial intelligence in university students: A recnoetic look. *REVISTA BOLETÍN REDIP,* 172-178.

Gendron, Y., Andrew, J., & Cooper, C. (2022). The perils of artificial intelligence in academic publishing. Critical Perspectives on Accounting, 87.

Judith Arnal, R. J. (2023). Artificial intelligence (i): the lesser "Brussels effect", the. Royal elcano institute.

Maldonado, F. J. (2023). The impact of artificial intelligence on academic and research papers. *Metropolitan Journal of Applied Sciences, vOLUME 6*(S1), 289-296.

Maria, C. (May 5, 2024). HubSpot. HubSpot: https://blog.hubspot.es/marketing/tipos-inteligenciaartificial#cinco

VERA, F. (2023). Integration of Artificial Intelligence in higher laEducation: Challenges and opportunities. Revista Electrónica Transformar, Vil-4(No. 1), 17-34.

Zhang, M., & Li, J. (2021). A commentary of GPT-3 in MIT Technology Review 2021. Fundamental Research, 1(6), 831-833.

MIX
Papier aus verantwortungsvollen Quellen
Paper from responsible sources
FSC® C105338

Printed by Books on Demand GmbH, Norderstedt / Germany